IT HAD TO BE GOD

(Blueprint for a life of thanksgiving)

KWABENA EDDIE MANKATA

DEDICATION

Beatrice Akuamoa – a granny who never ceases to amaze.
Ruby Okae-Asante – a warm and affectionate mother.
Nana kesewa Asante – a determined sister.
Steve Kwabena Asante – a great brother.

CONTENTS

The sovereign LORD has given me the capacity to be his spokesman, so that I know how to help the weary. He wakes me up every morning; he makes me alert so I can listen attentively as disciples do.

-Isaiah 50:4(NET)

ACKNOWLEDGMENTS

I am eternally grateful to God for my life. I am grateful for His insight and inspiration to write this book. Every day when I wake up I know for certain that His grace and mercy has brought me through.

I thank my siblings James, Evelyn, Vida, Bernice, Fred, Frank and Christian who have shaped my life in different ways. As the last the last born I am privileged to tap from your experiences. Next, I am indebted to Max, Cece, Martha, Akorfa, Selorm, Dorcas and Christiana for their daring love and support.

I thank Pastor Christian Tsekpoe for his inspiration. He is no doubt an unshakable pillar in the God's vineyard worth emulating.

And all the members of Pentecost International Worship Centre, Sakumono for their encouragement, thank you. To members of the two groups that have shaped my life and informed this book; Life Theatre and Royal Vine Theatre Ministries, God bless you.

I have been inspired by some selfless mentors and friends and if I am permitted to mention names without getting into trouble; Eugene Aikins, Kwesi Sekyere Asare,

1

Ovr. Richard Osei Mensah, Francis Osei Mensah, Eld Baffour Ofori Atta-Kena, Eld Edward Korely, Pr. Ovr. Ebenezer Afedzie, Anne Elemawusi Tawiah, Dcn Johnson Opoku Boateng, Samuel Offei Nartey, Shakirudeen Akiyemi, Justice Akwasi Sarpong, Bernard Mustapha Salifu, Dcn Alexander Boamoah Mensah and you whom I have regrettably left out, God bless you.

My acknowledgement will be incomplete without my inexplicable gratitude to Apostle Dr. Michael K. Ntumy for taking the time and patience off his busy schedules to read through the book, offer matchless suggestion and for writing the foreword for this book. Apostle God bless you and continually grant you wisdom.

I am grateful to Nehemiah K. Paul, Gabriel Agbagba, Selorm Aforla and Stephen Asante for reading through the book and offering fruitful remarks.

Christine Ofosu-Ampadu God bless you for the beautiful poem "Thank You." It simply summaries this book! Thanks to Joseph Bart-Plange for the cover and layout design.

Finally, thank you for reading this.

FOREWORD

In our present world, "Thank you" has become a very frequently used expression but woefully devoid of the sentiments of appreciation or gratitude it is meant to convey. It is more frequently used as an expression of courtesy after an exchange of greetings, at the end of phone conversations, letters or even having been reprimanded by one who has authority over us. "Thank you" in this sense has thus become a rote expression signifying nothing. This has been extended to actual circumstances when we want to express gratitude for a service or kindness done us. Frankly, many people go back to a benefactor to thank them because sheer politeness demands that.

What takes place at the interpersonal level has been transposed to the spiritual realm; between man and his God. Even worse than that is the fact that many do not acknowledge God as the Person of their gratitude. For some it is the State: the State provides them with jobs, money, shelter, healthcare and the security they need. They voted the administrators who govern them into power to do these things for them. If they do not deliver on their promises, they are voted out of office. Therefore such people think that politicians do not deserve our thanks. Worse still are those who make their fellow men, mere mortals, or idols, the objects of their thanksgiving.

To whom then do we owe gratitude or thanksgiving? How do we express our thanksgiving; when do we do it and why? Do we just multiply words to flatter the person, how sincere should we be and, how beneficial would this pattern of living benefit us?

The book you hold in your hand attempts to answer these questions. In *IT HAD TO BE GOD*, the author, Kwabena Eddie Mankata, a young business executive and highly involved church leader reminds the reader that God should be the object of our thanksgiving because it is to Him we owe everything. More than that Kwabena shows that thanksgiving must precede our every activity and that those who know this secret do not have to fret and bear needless pain in the hassles of this present life.

IT HAD TO BE GOD is written in simple, readable, contemporary language. The author does not concern himself with the theological and exegetical aspects of thanksgiving. He illustrates from empirical methods and doses of Scripture to whet the reader's appetite to pray—everywhere, every time, every day and for everything, even when the odds seem to be against us. If you are motivated to do this, his objective for writing this book would have been achieved.

APOSTLE DR MICHAEL NTUMY
Former Chairman, The Church of Pentecost
Former President, Ghana Pentecostal Council

INTRODUCTION

It was going to be the request that would completely turn my prayer life around. It was in the late hours of a Friday evening and what had driven me to pray at Paa Joe Annex (The Prayer ground behind Independence Hall; Kwame Nkrumah University of Science and Technology, Kumasi Ghana) was not a passion for prayer but a grave pressing need. No sooner had I started than, I heard a clear voice, "Thanksgiving is what motivates me to do more and that's all I ask of you tonight." What? I was disappointed that my tall list of requests had been substituted for one of thanksgiving. Thanksgiving for all I had already enjoyed when I needed nothing short of a miracle the next day.

There is always a satisfaction derived from pouring requests unto the Lord knowing you have shifted the burden to Him, and I wasn't going to enjoy one that evening. So I obeyed and to my surprise, I discovered a higher satisfaction from long hours of just thanking God. Besides, I had overwhelming miracles the subsequent days. I later on discovered something deeper when I understood the lyrics of the song, "He's already done enough" by Beverly Crawford. And for what David said below, I developed a deeper passion for thanksgiving.

1 [A Psalm] of David. Bless the LORD, O my soul: and all that is within me, [bless] his holy name.
2 Bless the LORD, O my soul, and forget not all his benefits:
3 Who forgiveth all thine iniquities; who healeth all thy diseases;
4 Who redeemeth thy life from destruction; who crowneth thee with lovingkindness and tender mercies;
5 Who satisfieth thy mouth with good [things; so that] thy youth is renewed like the eagle's.
Psalm 103: 1-5

One would expect thanksgiving to be done with understanding and passion because of concrete evidences. We wake up and have most, if not all the sensory organs functioning; we have material possessions. We are strategically placed, gifted and talented and practically good at something. There is something that even the poorest human on earth can be thankful for. Yet we have allowed all the wrong reasons, perceptions and our ignorance of scripture in all situations reduce our thanks to some few repetitive words that we pay little or no attention to.

When you come to the point of understanding that all you are, all you know, all you have and all you can be had to be God and not some sheer chance of your prowess, thanking God will not be an obligation but a thing of joy to do.

Even when you lack, you will find reasons to thank God because of the certainty of His divine provision according to His riches in glory (Phil 4:19). Irrespective of what confronts you, the Prophet Isaiah gives us reasons to thank God.

2 When you pass through the waters, I am with you; when you pass through the streams, they will not overwhelm you. When you walk through the fire, you will not be burned; the flames will not harm you.

Isaiah 43:2(NET)

Once you are breathing, the scripture "let everything that has breathe praise the LORD" applies to you. Thanksgiving ought to come from the heart and be so sincere that it puts smiles on the face of God. Even humans enjoy being appreciated how much more God. For when God is joyful we have strength (Nehemiah 8:10).

God cares about us so much. Of all His creation, man definitely stands out because we were created in His image and likeness. And He has given us dominion as well as provided for us all we will ever need.

3 When I consider thy heavens, the work of thy fingers, the moon and the stars, which thou hast ordained;

4 What is man, that thou art mindful of him? and the son of man, that thou visitest him?

5 For thou hast made him a little lower than the angels, and hast crowned him with glory and honour.

6 Thou madest him to have dominion over the works of thy hands; thou hast put all [things] under his feet:

7 All sheep and oxen, yea, and the beasts of the field;

8 The fowl of the air, and the fish of the sea, [and whatsoever] passeth through the paths of the seas.

9 O LORD our Lord, how excellent [is] thy name in all the earth!

Psalm 8:3-8

The definition of thanks for the purpose of this book will be gratitude for something received. However, there are portions of this book that will ask you to give thanks in hope of receiving something and that isn't any contradiction but a move of faith. What is more, it works!

As you walk through the pages of this book, I pray that the Holy Spirit speaks to your heart and stirs your spirit to gain deeper insights into thanksgiving. I pray you are inspired to thank God on two occasions; when you feel like it and when you don't. Be inspired!

.

1 WHY THANK GOD

Make your thanksgiving loud and your murmurings (if any) silent. Always remember that "God has two dwellings; one in heaven, and the other in a meek and a thankful heart – Isaak Walton

I have come to thank God with an understanding that brings me to my knees, virtually reduce me to nothing and ascribe the glory of every little achievement to Him. I thank God that all I have, all I know, all I can do, all I am and yet to be, had to be and will be Him. I strongly believe thanksgiving should be part of our everyday lives.

FOR WHO HE IS
1 O give thanks unto the LORD; for he is good and his mercy endureth forever
Psalm 118:1

Worship is appreciating God for who He is and thanksgiving is for what He has done. Yet it makes no error to thank God for who He is. God is loving, kind, gracious, merciful, faithful, understanding, compassionate, slow to anger, trustworthy and punctual just to mention a few.

Certainly there have been several moments in your life

9

that if it hadn't been one of His attributes you would have been dead.

If God could be robbed of His attributes, our lives would be miserable. In short, we would have been wiped out. In Ghana's political setting, whenever any ruling party loses an election, it has almost become a norm for the incoming party to prosecute and jail the outgoing party's officials under a broad offence titled "causing financial loss to the state." Every transaction is scrutinized to the last penny and a simple oversight or signature with the wrong pen is liable of warranting an arrest.

It has almost become a thing of revenge than holding officials accountable. I wonder for a moment what will happen to us if Jesus could be voted out. How miserable we will be. After all the prayers against the devil, the soul winnings and deliverance we would be good as dead if the devil took over. Even the devil desired to be worshipped. He was determined to give Jesus everything if Jesus would bow and worship him (Matt 4:9). The devil doesn't mind forfeiting everything just to be worshipped. He desires that power but thank God Jesus didn't worship him.

However thank God the bible says Jesus is the same yesterday, today and forever (Hebrews 13:8). Of all the attributes and characteristics of God, the very one I always adore is His eternal reign. If the devil could overthrow Jesus even for a day or two, we would lose every grace, favor and love. The eternal reign of God over everything in heaven, on earth and under the earth completely awes me and I thank Him for that. We have to thank God for who He is and that to me is a good enough reason You should too.

ALIVE

22 It is of the LORD's mercies that we are not consumed, because his compassion fail not.

23 They are new every morning; great is his faithfulness.
Lamentation 3:22-23

Whether saved or unsaved, the indisputable fact is you are alive because God said so. I don't know what people will make you believe or what you think yourself. It had to be God giving you breathe every single day. The song writer captured it beautifully with the lyrics, *"Your grace and mercy, brought me through. I'm living this moment because of you. I want to thank you and praise you too. Your grace and mercy brought me through."*

I have lived long enough to discover that every single disease is a potential life taker. Simple headache that seems to cower with an aspirin can kill as well as a tummy upset. Many people have died on the same operation tables others survived though the operations were carried out by the same group of surgeons for the same disease. I thank God to have survived different illnesses since birth.

I thank God that my health doesn't depend on me but Him. His divine health is made available daily. The doctors may have performed the operation but He supervised it. The prescription drug may have alleviated the pain but it was because of His stripes (Isaiah 53:5). Between the times I was shivering and when I woke up strong came God's divine healing.

There are too many testimonies of people who were declared clinically dead, and sent home to die but God touched them. They outlived their doctors. I have learnt to thank God for surviving every illness and you ought to do same.

It was no skill of the pilot or driver that got you to your destination. More experienced drivers behind impeccable modes of transportation have been involved in fatal accidents. Don't attribute it to chance or luck; *it had to be God* for you to come out unscathed.

Even if you lost a limb or were deformed in anyway, you have more reason to thank God because better short of a limb than death. People travel shorter and longer distances than you do every day and have died, yet God keeps you! You are alive because of God's grace. Simple truth!

3 When Paul had gathered a bundle of brushwood and was putting it on the fire, a viper came out because of the heat and fastened itself on his hand.

4 When the local people saw the creature hanging from Paul's hand, they said to one another, "No doubt this man is a murderer! Although he has escaped from the sea, Justice herself has not allowed him to live!"

5 However, Paul shook the creature off into the fire and suffered no harm.

6 But they were expecting that he was going to swell up or suddenly drop dead. So after they had waited a long time and had seen nothing unusual happen to him, they changed their minds and said he was a god.

Acts 28:3-6 (NET)

Paul was expected to die and when he didn't, he earned the status of a god. *It had to be God* he didn't die. There are many situations we have found ourselves in where people expected us to die but we survived. Sometimes people set traps for us; poison our foods, tamper with our vehicles, hide fetish stuffs under our desks and chairs at work and set armed robbers on us hoping we will die as a result yet we still live.

Many a time, while we sleep a lot of demonic activities go on but God ensures that we make it to next day because He neither sleeps nor slumbers. It doesn't make it a formality to wake up the next day. It is often said the richest place on earth is the cemetery. It houses the rich, gifted and creative minds some whom barely made their influence felt on earth. We are alive because of God. David captures it so well in the Psalms below;

1A Song of degrees of David. If [it had not been] the LORD who was on our side, now may Israel say;

2 If [it had not been] the LORD who was on our side, when men rose up against us:

3 Then they had swallowed us up quick, when their wrath was kindled against us:

4 Then the waters had overwhelmed us, the stream had gone over our soul:

5 Then the proud waters had gone over our soul.

6 Blessed [be] the LORD, who hath not given us [as] a prey to their teeth.

7 Our soul is escaped as a bird out of the snare of the fowlers: the snare is broken, and we are escaped.

8 Our help [is] in the name of the LORD, who made heaven and earth.

Psalm 124

Dear reader, life may not have been fair to you. You might have been disadvantaged; might be dealing with issues that seem to overwhelm you but the struggle means you are not defeated yet. A living dog is indeed better than a dead lion (Eccl. 9:4). There's hope that at the scent of water a cut tree will sprout again. How much more a human being? Being alive is necessary for hope.

Every single day you wake up is a miracle. Every day you hear from your relations living far and near is a miracle. Every day your unsaved friends and loved ones wake up is a bigger miracle because another opportunity is presented for them to be saved. *It had to be God* you are alive to read this book. Thank God for your life now.

We have not reached our destinations but thank God we are not where we used to be. We have grown, gained experiences and come very far in this life. The sums of our different experiences have shaped us into better Christians. There are innocent people wallowing in prison; mad men on the streets and in hospitals; blind, deaf and dumb, physically deformed in a way; some of whom are our age mates or even younger but should we count ourselves fortunate or lucky? No! *It had to be God.*

If you have ever visited the accident units, intensive care units, burns and other units at any hospital in the country, your abilities to breath alone, blink or even appreciate taste will drive you to thank God. When you wake up, it is your cue to thank God.

SAVED
8 For it is by grace that you have been saved, through faith- and this is not from yourselves, it is a gift of God.
9 Not of works, so that no one can boast."
Ephesians 2:8-9(NIV)

One day I heard Bishop Noel Jones preach about the grace of God. He likened it to someone drowning in sea and in order to be saved raises the hand to another who grabs it and pulls him out. The hand that is raised is faith and the hand that grabs it is grace. The truth is that the hand can be raised to the highest heights but if there's no hand to grab and pull, the person will drown.

You can have all the faith but if there's no grace you are doomed. Yet, even if you are too messed up or weak to raise your hand, grace can reach out to you and pull you out. Grace is the ultimate.

We are saved by grace not by any good works. I thank God that my salvation depends on Him and not my abilities and actions. I am not saved by being good but it is by grace. Had it not been for the saving grace of God, we would have perished by now.

Salvation began on the foundation of love. God loved the world and that's why He gave His only begotten son that whosoever believes in Him should not perish but have everlasting life (John 3:16).

What moved God in the first place to reconcile mankind to Him was love. And the depth of that love can't be conceived or proved, for while we were yet sinners, God demonstrated His love towards us and sent Christ to die for us (Rom 5:8 NIV). The Apostle Paul expanded on the inexplicable nature of God's love in the text below.

38 For I am persuaded, that neither death, nor life, nor angels, nor principalities, nor powers, nor things present, nor things to come.

39 Nor height nor depth, nor any other creature, shall be able to separate us from the love of God, which is in Christ Jesus our Lord"

Romans 8:38-39

Personally I see prayer as a love gift from God. The fact that you can call on Him no matter where you are, how you are feeling regardless of what you have even done and still have the assurance that He is listening is enough proof of love! God doesn't confuse a request and that amazes me more than anything. On a typical Sunday morning an assumption of billions of people send prayer requests to God. Some sing and write, others shout or speak undertone while others keep silent yet with expectations. And God delivers at an impeccable timing. He has never confused a request or found one too bulky or impossible to meet. The provision of a medium through which we can talk to God is enough reason to bless Him.

I thank God that my life depends on His righteousness and not mine. All our righteousness is like filthy rags before God (Isaiah 64:6). I have faced many trials and failed; many temptations and fell but haven't lost my salvation. There are times we fall into sin and are deserted by our loved ones. Sometimes we are left to hang out dry. It took God for us to find our feet. His compassion do not fail and are new every morning. The death of Jesus on the cross has made it possible for me to confess any time I fall short of His glory. I have the assurance that I'm forgiven anytime I confess my sins (1 John 9). Thank God for the blood Jesus shed on the cross at Calvary.

1 Abraham journeyed from there to the Negev region and settled between Kadesh and Shur. While he lived as a temporary resident in

Gerar,

2 Abraham said about his wife Sarah, "She is my sister." So Abimelech, king of Gerar, sent for Sarah and took her.

3 But God appeared to Abimelech in a dream at night and said to him, "You are as good as dead because of the woman you have taken, for she is someone else's wife."

4 Now Abimelech had not gone near her. He said, "Lord, would you really slaughter an innocent nation?

5 Did Abraham not say to me, 'She is my sister'? And she herself said, 'He is my brother.' I have done this with a clear conscience and with innocent hands!"

6 Then in the dream God replied to him, "Yes, I know that you have done this with a clear conscience. That is why I have kept you from sinning against me and why I did not allow you to touch her.

7 But now give back the man's wife. Indeed he is a prophet and he will pray for you; thus you will live. But if you don't give her back, know that you will surely die along with all who belong to you."

Gen 20: 1-7

In the scripture above, Abraham had lied about Sarah. In fairness to King Abimelech, he would have committed no sin in sleeping with Sarah. As a matter of fact in verse four of the above text, Abimelech argued his case out with the Lord because he and his nation were innocent and Abraham was the one who deserved to be punished. I love God's response to him

6 Then in the dream God replied to him "Yes, I know that you have done this with a clear conscience. That is why I have kept you from sinning against me and why I did not allow you to touch her."

God kept him from sinning! One of the many reasons we must thank God is He has kept us from many sins. God has kept you and me from many troubles not because we were strong-willed or smart. *It had to be God* who placed within us some restraint. It was God who made us stay up all night thinking about some other issues rather than focusing on whatever sin that laid near us. It was God that distracted us else we would have been in jail by now. The reason you didn't sleep with the man or woman was God. The reason you refused to go along with your friends who ended up in trouble was God. The reason you didn't touch that deal was God. The reason you took a U-turn was God. The reason you didn't cheat in that exam was God. *It had to be God* who kept us from sinning.

3 But the Lord is faithful, who shall establish you, and keep [you] from evil.
2Thess 3:3

It had to be God holding us together till now. *It had to be God* we are saved. You need to pause and thank Him for a few minutes before reading on.

Salvation, one would think is enough display of God's love but it isn't. There is heaven. A place our minds and hearts will never understand its overwhelming beauty and glory! A place devoid of pain, suffering and tears! Every struggle will end. Every battle will be won. Every need will be met.

4 And God shall wipe away all tears from their eyes; and there shall be no more death, neither sorrow, nor crying, neither shall there be any more pain: for the former things are passed away.
Revelation 21:4

What fascinates me is the fact that we will be with the Lord every single moment of every day, to enjoy His awesome presence and have a chat with Him face to face. S. J. Hill said *"Consider the Garden of Eden. Can you imagine the intoxicating fragrance of God that Adam and Eve experienced as they walked with Him and enjoyed the beauty of a newly made world? Can you picture the love and passion among the three of them? This was what Adam and Eve were created for: perfect relationship with the Father. They not only felt His presence; they walked in His presence. They experienced Him."* That is the experience prepared for us. I am grateful to God for heaven. Read below how the bible describes the new heaven.

1 And I saw a new heaven and a new earth: for the first heaven and the first earth were passed away; and there was no more sea.

2 And I John saw the holy city, new Jerusalem, coming down from God out of heaven, prepared as a bride adorned for her husband.

3 And I heard a great voice out of heaven saying, Behold, the tabernacle of God [is] with men, and he will dwell with them, and they shall be his people, and God himself shall be with them, [and be] their God.

4 And God shall wipe away all tears from their eyes; and there shall be no more death, neither sorrow, nor crying, neither shall there be any more pain: for the former things are passed away.

5 And he that sat upon the throne said, Behold, I make all things new. And he said unto me, Write: for these words are true and faithful.

6 And he said unto me, It is done. I am Alpha and Omega, the beginning and the end. I will give unto him that is athirst of the fountain of the water of life freely.

7 He that overcometh shall inherit all things; and I will be his God, and he shall be my son.

8 But the fearful, and unbelieving, and the abominable, and murderers, and whoremongers, and sorcerers, and idolaters, and all liars, shall have their part in the lake which burneth with fire and brimstone: which is the second death.

9 And there came unto me one of the seven angels which had the seven vials full of the seven last plagues, and talked with me, saying, Come hither, I will shew thee the bride, the Lamb's wife.

10 And he carried me away in the spirit to a great and high mountain, and shewed me that great city, the holy Jerusalem, descending out of heaven from God,

11Having the glory of God: and her light [was] like unto a stone most precious, even like a jasper stone, clear as crystal;

12 And had a wall great and high, [and] had twelve gates, and at the gates twelve angels, and names written thereon, which are [the names] of the twelve tribes of the children of Israel:

13 On the east three gates; on the north three gates; on the south three gates; and on the west three gates.

14 And the wall of the city had twelve foundations, and in them the names of the twelve apostles of the Lamb.

15 And he that talked with me had a golden reed to measure the city, and the gates thereof, and the wall thereof.

16 And the city lieth foursquare, and the length is as large as the breadth: and he measured the city with the reed, twelve thousand furlongs. The length and the breadth and the height of it are equal.

17 And he measured the wall thereof, an hundred [and] forty [and] four cubits, [according to] the measure of a man, that is, of the angel.

18 And the building of the wall of it was [of] jasper: and the city [was] pure gold, like unto clear glass.

19 And the foundations of the wall of the city [were] garnished with all manner of precious stones. The first foundation [was] jasper; the second, sapphire; the third, a chalcedony; the fourth, an emerald;

20 The fifth, sardonyx; the sixth, sardius; the seventh, chrysolite; the eighth, beryl; the ninth, a topaz; the tenth, a chrysoprasus; the eleventh, a jacinth; the twelfth, an amethyst.

21 And the twelve gates [were] twelve pearls; every several gate was of one pearl: and the street of the city [was] pure gold, as it were transparent glass.

22 And I saw no temple therein: for the Lord God Almighty and the Lamb are the temple of it.

23 And the city had no need of the sun, neither of the moon, to shine in it: for the glory of God did lighten it, and the Lamb [is] the light thereof.

24 And the nations of them which are saved shall walk in the light of it: and the kings of the earth do bring their glory and honour into it.

25 And the gates of it shall not be shut at all by day: for there shall be no night there.

26 And they shall bring the glory and honour of the nations into it.

27 And there shall in no wise enter into it anything that defileth, neither [whatsoever] worketh abomination, or [maketh] a lie: but they which are written in the Lamb's book of life.
Rev 21:1-27

Imagine for a moment such beauty! I just wish I could bump into the idea bank from which God drew his know how to put up the perspective of Heaven as described in the above revelation.

Augustine said *"Men go abroad to wonder at the height of mountains, the huge waves of the sea, the long course of rivers, the vast compass of the ocean, the circular motion of the stars but they pass by themselves and don't even notice".*

We are most times fascinated by skyscrapers, mansions, castles, bay-end-gable and landscapes. We wonder how the architects came up with such audacious ideas and how they made it work. If these men were inspired and could put up these mansions, do you have any idea what God can come up with? Do you? I can't even imagine. I know we will be completely blown away when we get there.

There is only one way to get there. Jesus is the answer and you have to accept him as your Lord and personal savior to gain access to this unimaginable setting of love. It is either *heaven* or *hell* and I implore you to make the choice today. Jesus is the way, the truth and the life and none shall come to the father except by Him. Confess your sins today and accept Him. God wants us to enjoy life on earth and also make it to heaven so He provides us with a manual; the bible. It is the only book inspired by God carefully written to contain solutions to all problems under the sun. The scriptures can't be broken and it has and will live longer than any book. The word of the Lord abides forever and every word in it will be fulfilled.

16 All Scripture is God-breathed and is useful for teaching, rebuking, correcting and training in righteousness.
2 Timothy 3:16(NET)

The bible is a reason to thank God. Sometimes it is amazing how God can lead you to a scripture that works for a particular situation you find yourself in. There is nothing new under the sun and every misfortune we are confronted with has a similar or far worse situation in the bible for which we can apply the needed solution. The bible isn't reserved for a few but for all. I am grateful to God for the bible.

And then there is the Holy Ghost our sweet comforter who directs our paths and comforts us moment by moment. When we don't even know how to pray, the Holy Spirit makes intercessions for us through groaning that cannot be uttered. There are countless moments in my life when His counsel has proved perfect in the midst of confusion when I obeyed. He has given directions on what to say, where to go and how to go about it. Personally the Holy Ghost is a priceless gift and if you have not experienced Him, I implore you to do so and begin thanking God for Him (Holy Spirit).

RELATIONSHIPS - FAMILY AND FRIENDS

9 Two [are] better than one; because they have a good reward for their labour.

10 For if they fall, the one will lift up his fellow: but woe to him [that is] alone when he falleth; for [he hath] not another to help him up.

11 Again, if two lie together, then they have heat: but how can one be warm [alone]?

12 And if one prevail against him, two shall withstand him; and a threefold cord is not quickly broken.

Eccl 4:9-12

I have learnt over the years that relationships do not come with obligations contrary to what people may say. Relationships come with opportunities. Opportunities to know people better, appreciate their differences; to share a joke, discuss ideas and work together. Opportunities to divide our grief and double our joy! When we see it the other way round, it becomes a burden to hold any relationship at all.

I love my family. We each bring to the table something beautifully unique. Some people wish they belonged to different families or were raised by different people because they do not appreciate the composition of their families. You might have a genuine reason to hate your family but God placed you in there for a reason and when you discover it, not only would you appreciate your family but you would thank God for them.

Family blesses us in more than we know. Sometimes a secret prayer from someone we detest so much might be what is holding us up. Kind words and unseen gestures are always going on in families. Reunions and parties of all kinds on occasions embolden our sense of belongingness no doubt. Even those relatives with messed up lifestyles may be a burden yet it teaches us to be closer to God and not end up like them. They teach us to trust God to turn their lives around.

There is no ideal and perfect family under the sun. The families you wished you belonged to are battling problems yours can't handle. They seem to have it all together but should God reveal their covered situations, you will bless God for yours. Whatever family you have, God has been good to you because a lot of things have happened since you were born till date, that if it hadn't been for them, you would have been worse off. Thank God for your family.

If you are married and you have kids or not, thank God. The fact that you are married is enough reason to thank God. To have married the love of your life is too good a reason. Many wish to hold the title of a "Mrs." but haven't yet. Every marriage has problems and that shouldn't blind you from appreciating the miracle you are married to. Spouses shape lives in a way no one else can. Even the meanest and most ungrateful spouse is a child of

God with a long rope and when you begin to see things in this other way, God will work things out. The people enjoying their marriages never missed a chance to thank God for their spouses and you can begin to enjoy yours if you trust God to work things out. A cord of three strands is not easily broken.

If you are single, you have reason to thank God. Across the nation every day especially on weekends, a lot of marriage ceremonies are being conducted and as surely as the Lord lives, it shall be your turn one day. God does all things beautiful in His own time. Keep thanking God for the special spouse that awaits you and the unique marriage yours would be.

You better start thanking Him for your children too. They are gifts and though sometimes you wish to return them for a day or two, you can testify that they have blessed you more than ever. They have brought comfort and joy, a kind word, warmth with a hug and laughter just by being themselves. Children grow up to alleviate pain, even live the dreams of parents and give reasons to hold on to life. You got a child, it is a reason to thank God. And if you don't have a child, thanks might just get you one. But even if you don't get one, thank God anyway.

I have learnt to thank God for love, encouragement and support of friends who were once total strangers. I have always believed in the impeccable timings of God to bring into our lives people to help us through a storm in order for us to make it to shore. Every one under the sun is confronted with an issue. James, a servant of God and the Lord Jesus Christ admonishes us to carry each other's burden and pray for one another (James 5: 16). All of us have burdens and I believe God in His infinite wisdom designed life in such a way to make us not only share ideas and suggestions, but more importantly recognize the need for one another and lend a helping hand whenever we can. This consequentially teaches us to love and care for one another. The truth is no matter how manly you appear, at one point in your life you will fail. You will need the help of another to make it to the end. I believe every single person God brings into our lives comes to build us up in a certain area specifically. I have had people who taught me a thing or two in finance; others shaped my career; some helped me deal with bad habits; others too scarred their knees interceding for me. All of them eventually helped me grow spiritually in God in a way including the ones who hurt and disappointed me. Those who walked out leaving a gap yet to be filled taught me how I needed to appreciate people more. Every single acquaintance is a blessing in disguise. Thank God for all your friends.

Indeed a man's friends must show himself friendly; and there is a friend who sticks closer than a brother.
Proverbs 18:24(NKJV)

NEEDS AND POSSESSIONS
1 Then in the month of Nisan, in the twentieth year of King Artaxerxes, when wine was brought to me, I took the wine and gave it to the king. Previously I had not been depressed in the king's presence.

2 So the king said to me, "Why do you appear to be depressed when you aren't sick? What can this be other than sadness of heart?" This made me very fearful.

3 I replied to the king, "O king, live forever! Why would I not appear dejected when the city with the graves of my ancestors lies desolate and its gates destroyed by fire?"

4 The king responded, "What is it you are seeking?" Then I quickly prayed to the God of heaven

5 and said to the king, "If the king is so inclined and if your servant has found favor in your sight, dispatch me to Judah, to the city with the graves of my ancestors, so that I can rebuild it."

6 Then the king, with his consort sitting beside him, replied, "How long would your trip take, and when would you return?" Since the king was amenable to dispatching me, I gave him a time.

7 I said to the king, "If the king is so inclined, let him give me letters for the governors of Trans-Euphrates that will enable me to travel safely until I reach Judah,

8 and a letter for Asaph the keeper of the king's nature preserve, so that he will give me timber for beams for the gates of the fortress adjacent to the temple and for the city wall and for the house to which I go." So the king granted me these requests, for the good hand of my God was on me.

Neh 2:1-8 (NET)

Nehemiah was putting plans together to rebuild the broken walls of Jerusalem. He obviously needed some materials beyond his budget. He went into the presence of the king depressed and immediately the king inquired of his demeanor. Nehemiah quickly prayed to the Lord and gave a reply. I believe he prayed for wisdom to know what to say and for God to touch the king's heart. Since the heart of the king is in the Lord's hands like channels of water and He turns it wherever He wants (Prov. 21:1), Nehemiah made his request. The king granted his request because the gracious hand of the Lord was upon him. Nehemiah didn't say because he had connections or the King owed him a favor. He said because the gracious hand of the Lord was upon him.

God has been the provider of our needs since the foundation of the earth. Never has He forgotten to provide for the numerous fishes in the sea, birds in the air and all other animals on earth for even a day. He provides the plants and trees with water and sunlight. The birds neither sow nor harvest but He feeds them. His timing is simply impeccable. If you then, although you are evil, know how to give good gifts to your children, how much more will your Father in heaven give good gifts to those who ask Him! (Matt 7:11). God knows how to provide for His own.

Hard work rewards. Connections make way. Yet it is God's divine power that has bestowed on us everything necessary for life and goodliness through the rich knowledge of the One who called us by His own glory and excellence (2 Pet 1:3 NET). Every property we have, had to be God. Every need that is met had to be God! Not that we are sufficient of ourselves to think of anything as of ourselves; but our sufficiency is of God (2 Cor. 3:5).

When we receive gifts from people no matter the occasion, we show our appreciation in different forms. The kind of appreciation we show sometimes depends on the size or type of gift and how necessary the gifts meets our immediate needs. A newly married couple will send messages to all who gave gifts of a certain size, call those whose gifts are of a certain value and visit those whose gift are exceedingly big. It is our human nature. However, all these appreciation are only possible if they put their names and contacts behind the gifts.

A very important thing to note is that appreciation is shown to one whose name appears on the gifts and not the handlers or the carriers. The truth is that God gives us gifts every day without putting His name on it and because we don't know the source, we often times give thanks to the carrier of the gift. When we are knowledgeably informed in scriptures about God being the sole provider of life and all that pertains to it, we will be eternally grateful for every penny we receive whether we worked for it or not, whether we deserved it or not.

You can buy me a car or a house as a gift. I will thank you with all my heart but when I get home I will fall on my knees and bless God, because it had to be God. He touched you and you simply obeyed. I learnt from Bishop Jones that when your enemy blesses you, *it had to be God.* God is the provider of our needs. God is the provider of all possessions and properties. If you own one, *it had to be God!*

One day I got to the Kwame Nkrumah Circle main station at dawn and saw people sleeping on the bare floor, benches, and tables and in parked cars. I didn't have trouble wondering where or how they slept when it rained.

There and then I learned to appreciate God even for a pillow. Something more striking I observed is how soundly and deeply they slept. There are people living in mansions but sleep has eluded them. Without sleeping pills they are better off as security guards manning their own conscience. If you can sleep amidst the pressures, uncertainties and inadequacies *it had to be God.* For God grants sleep to those He loves (Psalm 127:2b NIV).

SUCCESSES AND ACHIEVEMENTS

1 A Song of degrees for Solomon. Except the LORD build the house, they labour in vain that build it: except the LORD keep the city, the watchman waketh [but] in vain.
Ps 127:1

Every day we chalk new successes. Whether in academics, business or ministry, we experience success whether seen or unseen. Every struggle we overcome, every deal we seal, every word we preach, every song we sing or every talent we use gives us successes no matter how inconspicuous they may be. Every achievement and milestone we get in life has God's invincible hand behind it. God has ordained us to become the head and not the tail (Deut 28:13). God gave ideas when we were confused in the middle of our endeavors. God opened the doors when we least expected. God created opportunities when we were ready to use our acquired skills. God is responsible for our successes and achievements. *It had to be God.*

We don't owe our success to our elegance and intelligence. There have been a lot of occasions where the Lord has directed me to specific topics to revise and having studied them well, I passed graciously. Even the ability to understand the question is a blessing in itself. There have been times where I thought I was going to fail but passed and times where I was so sure to pass but somehow failed. I cannot state with certainty what accounted for all that but all I know is every success in my academics at all levels had to be God. Everyone has a story when it comes to exams, theses and term papers. Even the opportunity to have accessed some level of education till now had to be God!

As an entrepreneur, I know how well proposals have to be drafted to win contracts. You have to scrutinize to the minutest details all statements and figures before sending it through the mail if you are to stand any chance at all of being awarded the contract. Most times you get bullied by the giants and favorites in the field and it takes the grace of God to win some. It takes an idea or strategy given by God to get it right. Some I have won. Success in any business venture needs strategies and action plans but it takes the grace of God to access success in business. All the successes we have in our businesses both personal and otherwise had to be God. He stepped in and I know so.

Every day we are presented with new challenges in different forms. Some could be life threatening or one we could win with ease. Some battles we have won and others we have lost. Every battle we had ever won, challenges we overcame had to be God. May I submit to you that we could have won all if we had trusted God enough! We prevailed because of God, for by strength shall no man prevail (1 Sam 2:9).

Now the reason we have become so daring is because we know if God be for us who can be against us? (Roman 8:31) Even in our weakest state, we made some appreciable breakthroughs because God was on our side. We may have been prepared with all the strategies and tactics but the victory came from the Lord.

31 The horse is prepared for the day of battle but the victory is from the LORD.
Proverbs 21:31 (NET)

POSITIONS/STATUS

27 But God chose what the world thinks foolish to shame the wise, and God chose what the world thinks weak to shame the strong.

28 God chose what is low and despised in the world, what is regarded as nothing, to set aside what is regarded as something,

29 so that no one can boast in his presence.

30 He is the reason you have a relationship with Christ Jesus, who became for us wisdom from God, and righteousness and sanctification and redemption,

31 so that, as it is written, "Let the one who boasts, boast in the Lord.

1Cor 1:27-31 (NET)

Today we hold positions and have titles we never imagined we could hold and have respectively. Some of the positions we hold, we were the least people qualified for our current position but God made it possible. God took us from a remote setting and set our feet on high pedestals. Some of us till date remain the most educated and well placed members in our entire extended families. To a large extent we have been more favored than others in our families. Our hometowns haven't seen anybody as educated or talented as we are. The promotion could only have come from God, not from the east or west or south. He set someone down and took you up there (Psalm 75:6-7).

The positions we hold in our organizations could have been given to hundred other people. As a matter of fact we did apply with over hundred other people. About forty passed the aptitude test and ten passed the first interview. Three people remained. One had all the qualification and the other had all the experience yet you got the job. You might think you performed well at the interview; maybe you did yet it was God who gave you an idea and the sharp retentive memory. You might have even failed the interview but God did it for you anyway. No matter how stressful your job is, once you wake up to one, you have a reason to thank God. If you own a company too, no matter its stage and size or your struggle you ought to start thanking God for the idea and sustenance till now.

People of all ages now respect us. They value our opinions highly simply because God has blessed us in a way. When Job was anointed and had a relationship with God, he confessed there was nothing he couldn't do. He commanded respect and was highly regarded by all men.

Examine carefully the chapter below

1 Then Job continued his speech:

2 "O that I could be as I was in the months now gone, in the days when God watched over me,

3 when he caused his lamp to shine upon my head, and by his light I walked through darkness;

4 just as I was in my most productive time, when God's intimate friendship was experienced in my tent,

5 when the Almighty was still with me and my children were around me;

6 when my steps were bathed with butter and the rock poured out for me streams of olive oil!

7 When I went out to the city gate and secured my seat in the public square,

8 the young men would see me and step aside, and the old men would get up and remain standing;

9 the chief men refrained from talking and covered their mouths with their hands;

10 the voices of the nobles fell silent, and their tongues stuck to the roof of their mouths.

11 "As soon as the ear heard these things, it blessed me, and when the eye saw them, it bore witness to me,

12 for I rescued the poor who cried out for help, and the orphan who had no one to assist him;

13 the blessing of the dying man descended on me, and I made the widow's heart rejoice;

14 I put on righteousness and it clothed me, my just dealing was like a robe and a turban;

15 I was eyes for the blind and feet for the lame;

16 I was a father to the needy, and I investigated the case of the person I did not know;

17 I broke the fangs of the wicked, and made him drop his prey from his teeth.

18 "Then I thought, 'I will die in my own home, my days as numerous as the grains of sand.

19 My roots reach the water, and the dew lies on my branches all night long.

20 My glory will always be fresh in me, and my bow ever new in my hand.'

21 "People listened to me and waited silently; they kept silent for my advice.

22 After I had spoken, they did not respond; my words fell on them drop by drop.

23 They waited for me as people wait for the rain, and they opened their mouths as for the spring rains.

24 If I smiled at them, they hardly believed it; and they did not cause the light of my face to darken.

25 I chose the way for them and sat as their chief; I lived like a king among his troops; I was like one who comforts mourners.

Job 29 (NET)

It had to be God for the people to treat Job in such manner. Every verse talks about either his ability to meet a need or divine wisdom being displayed! It had to be God. Our positions and status today is the doing of the Lord. I agree with the Psalmist when he said the Lord has done this and it is marvelous in our eyes (Psalm 118:23).

Everyone has a shocking survival story but the bottom line is God has brought us from a certain pit and placed our feet high. In our hopelessness, when we felt weak and sad, God chose us and for that matter we owe Him thanks. Our boast should be in the Lord as the Apostle Paul summed it up when he told the people of Corinth that let the one who boast, boast in the Lord. Before the Apostle

Paul the Prophet Jeremiah had remarked same.

23 *Let the one who boasts boast about this: that they have the understanding to know me that I am the LORD, who exercises kindness, justice and righteousness on earth, for in these I delight, declares the LORD*
Jeremiah 9:23 (NIV)

Sometimes we get into these positions and tend to exploit others. We become judgmental and treat others with disdain. When you see the evil in your own heart, the impureness of your thoughts and how well you have consciously fed the flesh yet grace and mercy wakes you up every morning, provide for you food, clothing and shelter and plead your case every now and then; you have no right to judge another because you are no better. It just had to be God. And you will be ready to assist people. You will keep your opinions and correct them in love.

One of my favorite deep thoughts reads *"Isn't it amazing that God who is all powerful and rich beyond measure is accessible irrespective of place and time yet when man comes to power and gains "small" riches, he becomes inaccessible? Learning from God, leadership is accessibility."* Let us make ourselves accessible and help out.

TALENTS AND SPIRITUAL GIFTS

17 *Every good gift and every perfect gift is from above, and cometh down from the Father of lights, with whom is no variableness, neither shadow of turning.*
James 1:17

Every single gift and talent we possess belongs to God. My definition of spiritual gifts is given by the Holy Ghost in the text below

7 *But the manifestation of the Spirit is given to every man to profit withal.*

8 For to one is given by the Spirit the word of wisdom; to another the word of knowledge by the same Spirit;

9 To another faith by the same Spirit; to another the gifts of healing by the same Spirit;

10 To another working of miracles; to another prophecy; to another discerning of spirits; to another [divers] kinds of tongues; to another the interpretation of tongues."

1 Corinthians 12: 7-10

The exercising of these gifts ease evangelism and helps depopulate the devil's kingdom. God literally comes down to work within us when we use our gifts. We are not blessed for being carriers of the gifts but for using them. And if for a moment you have benefited from these gifts whether as a vessel or the recipient, you owe God thanks.

Every now and then people dazzle us with the exhibit of their talents. Sometimes the display of our talents also generates comments from people which awe us. These gifts and talents have led us to important places and brought us before great men! (Proverbs 18:16). God saw a need in this world and created us with talents and gifts to meet those needs.

10 For we are God's workmanship; created in Christ Jesus to do good works, which God prepared in advance for us to do.

Ephesians 2:10 (NIV)

The question arises whether we are using it for what it was actually intended for or not. All the gifts and talents we possess, we didn't buy or work for them. It had to be God! He gave it to us freely and it is a good reason to thank Him.

It is amazing how most times we make it about ourselves. We walk in the prominence of our abilities beaming with pride. We want to be hailed and cajoled to use that which God gave to us for free. We do as we please, appear as and when we want, to the disadvantage of the body of Christ. Indeed, the gifts and call of God are irrevocable but we won't be rewarded for possessing the gifts but for using it. There are too many people who have lost the anointing backing their talents and gifts because they were not using it for God's glory. It had to be God you can sing so well, preach with much insight, write so well or exhibit so well the gifts and talents you possess. Don't make it about you. It has not, has never been and will never be about you. It's time to use it for His Glory.

MISFORTUNES

18 In everything give thanks; for this is the will of God in Christ Jesus concerning you.
1Thess 5:18

It doesn't make sense to thank God for the misfortunes we go through. Truth be told, it is the most difficult thing to do. It is so easy to preach it until you are confronted with a situation. For a moment the only word which seems to proceed out of our mouth is "why" and not thank you. What should I say to GOD when I trusted His divine healing to come forth, instead my loved one died? It makes no sense to thank Him when the exact opposite happens.

Albert Barnes said *"We can always find something to be thankful for and there may be reasons why we ought to be thankful for even those dispensations which appear dark and frowning."*

In all things we are supposed to give thanks to God because everything that happens to us is meant to shape our lives and build us up in the Lord. And we know that all things work together for good for those who love God, who are called according to His purpose (Romans 8:28 NET).

On many occasions, breakthroughs and new pathways are tied to the end of misfortunes but we hardly see beyond the pain. Unless we go through it we wouldn't get it. Sometimes God takes us through trials to tear us away from unnecessary acquaintances and attachments. Other times God allows someone to break our hearts as they walk out from a relationship to save us from a marriage of misery.

Neale Donald said *"Each circumstance is a gift and in each experience is a hidden treasure"*. Whether you lost a job or a loved one; lost huge sums of money or your property; your heart is broken or you have been taken advantage of; you were skipped for a promotion or fell into trouble you caused yourself, there is a hidden treasure. Your duty is to discover the hidden treasure. So you owe God praise for using a worse situation to teach or provide you with something.

One way that helps you thank God in such situations is to count your blessings; count what is left and see if you can name them. If you can't, which I know for sure, you just have to thank God. Whatever we go through will not last. Bible considers it a moment! I heard a friend define a moment as one-sixth of a second. Read this text below;

14Knowing that he which raised up the Lord Jesus shall raise up us also by Jesus, and shall present [us] with you.

15 For all things [are] for your sakes, that the abundant grace might through the thanksgiving of many redound to the glory of God.

16 For which cause we faint not; but though our outward man perish, yet the inward [man] is renewed day by day.

17 For our light affliction, which is but for a moment, worketh for us a far more exceeding [and] eternal weight of glory;

18 While we look not at the things which are seen, but at the things which are not seen: for the things which are seen [are] temporal; but the things which are not seen [are] eternal.

2Cor 4:14-18

TIMELY INTERVENTION

1 O give thanks unto the LORD, for [he is] good; for his mercy [endureth] forever.

2 Let the redeemed of the LORD say [so], whom he hath

redeemed from the hand of the enemy.
Ps 107:1-2

Another reason why we should thank God is for His timely interventions. There have been countless moments when I thought God wasn't coming through; when I felt I was on my own only for God to show up in the nick of time. Too often, I don't know why but it seems God's time of action is almost a few minutes later than my final time of expectation. It has made me appreciate the LORD's confession in the book of Isaiah.

8For my thoughts are not your thoughts, neither are your ways my ways, saith the LORD.
9For as the heavens are higher than the earth, so are my ways higher than your ways, and my thoughts than your thoughts."
Isaiah.55:8-9

All I know is *it had to be God* to have survived. We both cannot remember all of God's timely interventions in our lives but there are some which bring tears to our eyes and an inexplicable feeling of joy because we know for a fact if God hadn't come through, that would have been our end.

Again I agree with the Psalmist saying, the Lord had done this and it is marvelous in our eyes. God sent the resources through people just when we had exhausted all options and most at times through avenues we least expected. God brought just the right people, opened the right doors when we grew tired of hanging on and were about to let go. *It simply had to be God.*

Corrie Ten Boom shares a powerful story about God's timely intervention. It was during the time when she and her family were experiencing trials while attempting to shelter Jews in Nazi-occupied Holland. She said, "Papa, everything is getting too bad. If the police come for us, how will we know that God is with us?" He responded, "When we go on a trip, when do I give you the ticket?"

"Just before we get on the train, Papa," Corrie answered. Her father said, "that's right, you don't need your ticket until you are about to board the train. But I always give you your ticket in time." That is how God is. He always gives us what we need. He is never late. Listen to the song, "Never would I have made it without you" by Psalmist Marvin Sapp and you will get it.

The greatest feeling is that, He isn't done with us yet. There are more interventions coming our way and even if He doesn't show up; I have no trouble concurring with Beverley Crawford's song "If the Lord doesn't do anything else, He's already done enough." Yet the story of the three Hebrew boys in Babylon makes me understand that God will show up if I do not compromise. I know before this week ends, God is coming your way with a breakthrough. Pause and bless Him if you believe.

Every breath is a reason to thank God. Every trial is a reason to thank God. Every triumph is a reason to thank God. Every joy is a reason to thank God. Every pain is a reason to thank God. Every failure is a reason to thank God. Every achievement is a reason to thank God. Every new day is a reason to thank God.

2 WHY OUR THANKS LACK PASSION AND WORDS

Life without thankfulness is devoid of love and passion. Hope without thankfulness is lacking in fine perception. Faith without thankfulness lacks strength and fortitude. Every virtue divorced from thankfulness is maimed and limps along the spiritual road. - John Henry Jowett

Our thanks sometimes lack sincerity as much as words. We tend to pay little or no attention to what we say during thanksgiving sessions which oft are the first part of all prayer sessions. What is worse? There is no passion. No wonder we can sing a praise song and at the same time be buried deeply in thoughts. We can sing and still observe with delight how others dance to the same song. We can even clap and shout "Thank you Jesus" after the praise leader absent-mindedly.

In a typical prayer meeting we sometimes have to be sweet-talked to thank God and if the reason is not compelling enough we eventually stay mute till a song is raised and ends or the next prayer topic is given. Try to lead people to pray with a topic "let's thank God for our lives" and chances are that by the third minute they would be staring at you for the next topic. Why we thank God the way we do aren't farfetched and here are a few….

SIMPLY UNGRATEFUL

We are simply ungrateful. We can fast and spend hours buried in intensive prayers when we are overwhelmed with a life threatening situation, yet when God's cavalry arrives we spend less than two minutes thanking Him. We totally forget the pain we went through, the tears we shed behind closed doors and the humiliation we had to endure before God stepped in our situation. We wave goodbye at God till another need arises.

Now we don't share our testimonies but keep them to ourselves unless we consider them as "eye-brow raisers". Yet it is written that they overcame him by the blood of the Lamb and by the word of their testimony; and they loved not their lives unto death (Rev 12:11). Sometimes we have the tendency to forget the goodness of the Lord. They either get swamped up by the pressures or pleasures of life. David knew this so well and thus remarked "bless the Lord oh my soul and forget not all His goodness."

Ingratitude seems wired to our system and we have to consciously unwire it. I am yet to rate a thanksgiving that can equate the reason for which it was given. For what shall we render to the Lord for all his benefits towards us? We will take up the cup of salvation, and call upon of the LORD (Psalm 116:12-13).

YOU-OWE-ME-MENTALITY

Our ingratitude is sometimes born out of the "you-owe-me or I-deserve-it" mentality. In other words, the "it-is-your-duty" mindset we hold towards those who offer support or help us through situations reduces our appreciation to a few words with little or no passion.

"It is the duty of our parents to meet our most basic needs. Whether we are thankful for them or not; it is their duty!" "We didn't ask to be here, they agreed to keep the pregnancy". "It is no big deal when we forget or deliberately do not say thank you" "Why thank someone who returns a favor after they remembered that they owed us and fulfilled it?"

"It is scriptural that our offerings and donations at church or to a charitable organization qualify us for God's blessings. He is mandated to bless us, after all the bible says he who gives to the poor lends to the Lord (Proverbs 19:17). And so God is fulfilling His duty by blessing us. It is our right to be blessed. Why thank Him every now and then? Why is it necessary to begin every prayer session with a thanksgiving? Until that *why* is answered, anything goes!

WE ACHIEVED IT BY OURSELVES

The joy of passing an examination is inexplicable; especially when you weren't sure you would pass. Not only does it relieve you of the fear of failure, it brings confidence and gives an inspiration to forge ahead. As a student when you announce the results to your family, all forms of congratulatory messages and praises come pouring in, sometimes accompanied with gifts and hugs.

Oh, how we love to live such moments! In the midst of all these the teacher is unfortunately forgotten. The one who taught, broke down complex methods into simpler modules and created simple analyses to explain difficult theories for easy comprehension, is forgotten. The teacher who took the pain to correct the student over and over again never comes to mind let alone be appreciated.

Whiles we may be skeptical to observe that teachers are paid to impart knowledge; there's no amount of money worth their effort, patience and the sound pieces of advice before, in-between and after the lectures. People have contributed in so many ways to our growth in all spheres of our lives. We don't always see them but it is certain there's always a prayer being said, a word being put in and a way being paved for us. When we however attribute our success at all levels from academia, career, ministry and relationships to our own efforts which we sometimes do, we see no reason to appreciate the invisible Hand behind our achievements.

IGNORANCE

Ignorance of scripture accounts for many unacceptable behaviors of Christians for which ingratitude is part. We are destroyed for lack of knowledge (Hosea 4:6). If we are not clearly informed about the source of our strengths, knowledge and abilities, it is natural to assume that we achieve everything by ourselves. If we don't know about the saving grace of our Lord Jesus and all it pertains, if we have no reference of daily provisions, timely interventions and all, how then do we give Him thanks?

We mess up every now and then but for His mercies we live. We are wired to the divine plan of God which shapes us to fulfill our destinies on earth. And what's more, join Him in heaven. If we are ignorant, we are pitiful! I read one day that, the saddest moment in the life of an atheist, is when he gets something without his effort and wants to be grateful, but does not know who to thank. Ignorance is a miserable disease!

DEPRECIATING VALUE OF DAILY BLESSINGS

When something becomes consistent, it becomes expected. When it is expected, it loses the appreciation of its occurrence; perhaps even its beauty. Once I read a comment by a friend that said, "If you think it is the alarm clock that wakes you up every morning, put it by a corpse." When we think it is a laid down formality or principle that we wake up morning, we lose the reasons to thank God.

The ending verses of Luke Chapter 2 presents the scenario where the parents of the boy Jesus had travelled a whole day without realizing he wasn't following them. Did they assume he was in the company of kinsfolk and acquaintances, so they never turned for a moment to check on Him? And for a whole day too! The truth is Jesus always did follow every year when they went to Jerusalem for the feast of Passover but not this time.

When something always happen, it is difficult to assume it wouldn't happen, much more appreciate it when it is happening. We make bold statements into tomorrow as if our sheer confidence secures a place for us. How many times have we seen or read about people so full of life yet not make it to the next day.

The book of Luke Chapter 17 presents a story of a ten member leper association who had heard of the power of Jesus. When information reached them Jesus was passing their direction, I personally believed they planned a strategy. They positioned themselves well and waited for Jesus.

Their plan worked. They got the attention of Jesus and whiles carrying out his instructions, they got their healing. Only one of them came back to give glory to God and worshipped Jesus. A stranger! A Samaritan! The one who wasn't part of the lost sheep of Israel! Jesus was amazed at this man as the same time saddened by the absence of the other nine. God blesses us daily. Most times through our spouses, friends, loved ones, supervisors, relatives, colleagues and even strangers.

Owing to its daily occurrences, we tend to take them for granted because of familiarity We don't appreciate these people how much more God; the source and inspiration of these blessings. There are over seven billion people in the world and God has kept you alive still, irrespective of the fact that many prominent people have died. A laid down formality or a thoughtful display of agape love!? You decide!

3 KINDS OF THANKSGIVING

We would worry less if we praised more. Thanksgiving is the enemy of discontent and dissatisfaction. — Harry A. Ironside

Thanksgiving isn't only about words but singing, dancing and playing instrument; basically putting to use every gift and talent you possess to His glory. Moses and Miriam composed a thanksgiving song in Exodus 15 when God delivered them from the hands of the Egyptians. David said, I will sing unto the LORD, for he has been good to me (Psalm 13:6 NIV). Following no special order, these are kinds of thanksgiving I have put together.

EVERY DAY THANKS

This is what we do when God does something for us; even when we think we deserved it. From the time we wake up till we retire to bed, we have to thank God for the series of events that have unfolded in the day. An everyday thanks is supposed to be a ritual but done with understanding, passion and being mindful of words used. It is a ritual with creative effect. There are times I sing in the bath.

The song "Nyame ye Oh Nyame ye daa, sɛ w'ama ade akye yɛn bio…." (God is good. God is always good; for He has allowed us to see another day) has been my morning song. And whether it amuses you or not, the song "ɔma yɛn daa adziban, ɔyɛ yɛn ahiadze nyinaa Hallelujah Nyame te ase o daa… (He gives us our daily bread and meets our daily need, Hallelujah God is alive forever)" seems to come out of me when I am satisfied.

One of my mothers can't help but laugh anytime she hears me. You can find a thanksgiving song for every event in your life. As the name connotes everyday thanks, has to be done every day irrespective of the place and time.

THANKS IN ADVANCE

Advance thanks is thanks in the midst of trials. It is most difficult to do because everything around feels and looks worse. It is thanking God for what lies ahead when the current situation has no slight indication of changing. It is holding onto scriptures concerning your life. It is holding onto the God of impossibilities (Luke 1:37, 18:27) who knows the end from the beginning. It is birthed out of the truth that God loves you above all things and wants to be glorified through you.

Apostle Paul, writing to the Philippians told them he was confident that He who has begun a good work in them will perform it until the day of Jesus Christ (Phil 1:6). Every word of scripture will be fulfilled before Jesus comes and that includes the word concerning your life. The Song "Praise Him In Advance" by Psalmist Marvin Sapp has lyrics that say it all.

So go on ahead, right now thank God for the spouse and children yet to come. Thank Him for the new job, personal business and contracts. Thank God for the project. Thank God for the money you are expecting.

For even if earthly fathers who are evil know how to give good gifts to their children how much more God (Luke 11:13).

6 Be careful for nothing; but in everything by prayer and supplication with thanksgiving let your requests be made known unto God.

Phil 4:6

You may not feel like it, the odds may be against you, your body may not allow it, but do it anyway. Tell God, "I thank you that this situation is way over. I bless you I have found more than what I was looking for. You are far too kind. I am so grateful."

HIGHER THANKS

A higher form of thanksgiving is when we thank God for the success of another. When we learn to thank God for His blessings happening in the lives of our friends, families or even total strangers, God is assured that He would be acknowledged when He comes through with a blessing for us. Thanking God for another is an affirmation that we trust God to meet our needs once He has done it for someone.

It has shockingly become difficult if not impossible for Christians to thank God for the success of their fellow brethren. Envy and jealousy have usurped our sense of gratitude. Worse than envy and jealousy is when we attribute their success to corruption or even 'dirty blood money' for lack of words. We have become so cynical, questioning the breakthrough of other brethren. Sometimes we think we deserved better. Our attitude tends to question God about His criteria for blessings.

Sometimes we find everything wrong with the good people do because we hate them or they defy already existing tradition to help others out of certain situations. Instead of showing gratitude, we deepen our hatred for them and threaten to destroy them.

One time while Jesus was teaching about being the

good shepherd and how His sheep hears His voice and how He had the ability to give eternal life, the Jews took up stones to stone Him and He answered them saying..

32 "Many good works have I shewed you from my Father; for which of those works do ye stone me?"
John 10:32

We have to learn to thank God for the blessings of other people be it promotion, marriage, child birth, graduation etc. Your blessing has been dispatched already. Higher thanks will bring it. Remember your promotion comes from the Lord. We can practice higher thanks today.

TITHES, NORMAL AND FREE WILL OFFERING

Tithe I believe isn't only a requirement of a Christian but also a form of thanksgiving. I believe it is a way of showing appreciation for the monetary and material blessings God has brought our way. Tithing is more than fulfilling an obligation but is an opportunity to bless God and be blessed in return.

Offering takes many forms. Whether in cash or kind, offering is a kind of thanksgiving. It is a form of sacrifice unto the Lord not to atone for anything but to support the work of the LORD. When we understand that all we have was given to us by God, we wouldn't mind how much we put in the offering bowl. Simply because, God doesn't run out of resources and He can give us more than we give. I believe that how much we put in the offering bowl tells whether we trust God or not and whether we are selfish or not. We need to stop being emotional givers.

I learnt from Pastor Benny Hinn that giving shouldn't be based on how we are feeling, how the sermon touched us or how we woke up feeling in the morning. We have to give with an understanding not on our feelings.

Freewill offering has always been a thing of old and can

be found in Numbers 15. In my church, Pentecost International Worship Centre Sakumono, freewill offering is something we have understood so well. As the name connotes, it is freewill and not determined by anything but if I may be so bold to define it, I would say an offering defined by a measure of the appreciation of the goodness of the Lord. An offering we give voluntarily aside the offertory. We give it during praises, song ministrations by the choir or individuals, drama or choreography ministration, testimony sharing and prayer time. Also on occasions such as birthdays, marriage and naming, we give freewill offerings.

I can't find any reason for freewill than simply appreciating God and what is more, we are equally blessed and given back in good measure, pressed down, shaken together and running over. It might not be a practice in your church, but you can start practicing it today. Be Inspired!

4 MEAN WHAT YOU SAY

A good man out of the good treasure of his heart bringeth forth that which is good; and an evil man out of the evil treasure of his heart bringeth forth that which is evil: for of the abundance of the heart his mouth speaketh.
Luke 6:45

One day I was deeply touched as I listened to a friend preach on the theme, "Praise of the Heart." He said God is greater than great, wiser than wise, bigger than big and better than best. The English language is inadequate when it comes to thanking God, hence the essence of tongues-speaking. You do not understand the tongues but once your spirit man is lifted; you feel good. You are somehow satisfied you are telling God something beautiful.

I believe that although the English language seems inadequate, there are some words we can use. Some people have limited vocabulary when it comes to thanksgiving. They use the same words over and over again without thinking about them. Once there is a prayer session which normally begins with thanksgiving they will say the same things to God no matter how many times in a day the prayers are conducted. They have limited God to kindness, graciousness, faithfulness, and providence. There are some phrases they think aren't right to tell God, like "I can't live without you", "my mind, body and soul belong to you", "you have captured my heart", "I will do everything for you" and "I love you very much". They will rather tell the opposite sex. But does God appreciate such lovely words? Of course He does.

Consciously listen to yourself at the next prayer session and you would realize you are no different. Even the way we thank God is terrible. We do it with no passion at all. How will you feel if someone says thanks to you absentmindedly? I am sure angrier than if they had said nothing at all. What we say and how we say it tells a lot about how appreciative we are; for out of the abundance of the heart, the mouth speaks.

The Book of Psalms contains beautiful words from King David, the sons of Korah and the other authors. Their writings are so moving. Phrases like "you are my hiding place", "my secret refuge", "lover of my soul", "my one and only", "my light and salvation" among the lots are common to the book of Psalms. They understood that life was meaningless without God. He loves, creates, takes, gives, preserves, sustains, watches, understands, protects, guides, teaches, elevates, lights, destroys, builds, changes and so on.

One would think knowledge of the attributes of God permits us to have a set of unchanging vocabulary for thanksgiving, but it doesn't. His timely interventions alone should make us creative in finding words to thank Him. It is time to check your vocabulary! It's time to mean what you say and how you say it.

There's nothing under the sun that we can do or achieve by ourselves. Once you come to understand that God created everything and all you have was divinely orchestrated, you will fall on your knees with different words, so sweet and sincere that heaven will rejoice at your thanks. Your vocabulary however could be limited as a child's prayer but the sincerity of the words even in repetition is what I believe touches God.

And as Joyce Meyer said, a lot of people are thankful but don't take the next step to actually say it. They are thankful but don't give thanks. Unless you actually say it, your feelings about the appreciation won't be known. Take a bold step and tell God how grateful you are for everything He does for you.

5 WHEN TO THANK GOD

The greatest saint in the world is not the one who prays most or fast most; it is not he who gives most alms or is most eminent for temperance, chastity or justice; but is it he who is always thankful to God, who wills everything that God wills, who receives everything as an instance of God's goodness and has a heart always ready to praise God for it – William Law

In the United States and Canada, there is a day set aside as a national holiday tagged, "thanksgiving day" where they give thanks for the blessings of harvest and of the preceding year. It is celebrated on the fourth Thursday of November in the United States and on the second Monday of October in Canada. Roasted stuffed turkey has been associated with Thanksgiving Day.

A lot of us wait till the end of the year when we take stock of our lives to thank God for safely guarding us, our families, colleagues and friends. We wait till the last day of the last month in the year to offer our sacrifice of praise. Occasionally there are some Sunday services tagged "thanksgiving day" where we attempt to do nothing but thank God. Somehow we expect God to understand and wait till those services or moments to collect His due.

On other occasions, we thank God when we survive an accident, an illness and any near death experience. We then bid God goodbye till He delivers us again. Sometimes when an unexpected breakthrough or miracle comes our way, we find reason to pour a few words of appreciation to God.

Sometimes it takes the misfortunes of people for us to realize how merciful God has been. When people we know or even strangers suffer misfortunes that could have easily befallen us, we start counting our blessings. When we see people deformed in any way, we find reason to thank God for having the normal features and qualities of a human.

When so called events tagged "Acts of God" like tsunamis, earth quakes and heavy rains take place elsewhere, we find reason to thank God for not allowing us to experience such events.

We seem to be always waiting to escape something grave, experience a miracle or something to befall a neighbor before thanking God. How would you feel if all your appreciations are postponed till the end of the year? What if the joy that comes from being appreciated are heaped till the end of the year and shipped to you; when the motivation to do more is reserved for the 31st of December?

There is no season or time to thank God. When grace taps you saying, "wake up it is morning"; that is your cue to thank God. If you can see, feel, talk, read, hear, jump, walk, jog, clap, sleep, think or do anything in between, it's time to thank God. When you get home from work, it's time to thank God. Right now, you can pause and thank God for how far you, the family, the company, the church and this nation has come. Thanksgiving is the gate fee demanded at His presence (Ps 100:4).

[A Psalm] of David, when he changed his behaviour before Abimelech; who drove him away, and he departed. I will bless the LORD at all times: his praise [shall] continually [be] in my mouth.

Psalm 34:1

You can't be too late or early with thanksgiving. Every time is right to thank God.

6 BENEFITS OF THANKSGIVING

and as the magnet finds the iron, so it will find in every hour, some heavenly blessings - Henry Ward Beecher

Thanksgiving motivates anyone to give and do more. And if God is more gracious, loving and caring then I can only imagine what He will do for us when we thank Him. A thankful person is one focused on God. Thanksgiving says a lot about us to God.

We make mistakes and fall into sin, we lose loved ones, we lack and cry but one sure way to enjoy God is to live a life of thanksgiving. I realize even in the midst of all difficulty when you don't have the strength to spend even minutes in prayer, you can simply say those two words, thank you.

Thanksgiving is the gate fee to the presence of the Lord. The truth is God does not diminish or otherwise when we refuse to give Him thanks or vice versa.

While I am certain that God doesn't get discouraged or go through difficult moments and needs to be encouraged to feel good about Himself, thanksgiving gives Him joy. Knowing that the joy of the Lord is our strength (Nehemiah 8:10), I wonder why we wouldn't want to thank Him at all times.

When someone does something for you no matter how little or how well you deserved it, transform their day by giving thanks. Thanksgiving is a tremendous gift that can reassure someone and lighten their mood. If someone blesses you in a way, take time to tell them what they exactly did and encourage them.

A thankful heart can heal wounds, build and repair relationships. It has the potential to open doors on earth as well as in heaven.

I hope you are inspired enough to be a thanksgiving person. Take time to appreciate people but take a lot more time to appreciate God. Stay blessed. *It had to be God!*

Be Inspired!

TWO POEMS ON THANKSGIVING

THANKSGIVING CARD

Every card serves a unique purpose.

An Identity card (ID) provides an evidence of belonging to a department in a company, an association, a class and a nation. An ID card speaks for you and it grants you access to places you can't access even if you are known. It shows who you are

A business card does more than answer who are you but also more importantly what you do. It also shows your position in what you do, how to reach you and your business via location, phone or the web.

A money card (ATM, VISA, CREDIT, E-ZWICH) also answers who you are and why you can redraw money from your account. It gives you the opportunity to transact business on line and buy anything without having physical money. It is of course convenient and safer to carry

The health insurance card gives you access to a certain good degree of free medical care.

The Voter's ID gives you right to exercise your franchise

There are many kinds of cards and they all serve a particular purpose in life. But there is also a thanksgiving card.

The thanksgiving card does all of the above. It answers who why, how and what. The thanksgiving card is presented to God. It can be used at all times. The truth is if you learn to use it in your tough situation, it will get you out. Rather than wallowing in self-pity, murmuring and crying you can praise you way out of every situation with a thanksgiving card. When you thank God in advance for what you choose to experience, you are not only acknowledging that He is able but He is willing and has done it already.

It is the card you present before and after traveling

It is the card you present before and after securing a job

It is the card you present before and after a child is born

It is the card you present before and after winning a soul

It is the card you present before and after writing an exam

It is the card you present before and after winning a contract

It is the card you present before and after marriage ceremony

It is the card you present before and after gaining an admission

It is the card you present before and after undergoing an operation

It is simply the card you present before you sleep and when you wake up

I believe everyone has a thanksgiving card so far as you are saved but not everyone uses it. We have an inherent involuntary ability to see wrong in situation and not to show gratitude for things in life. We are sometimes forgetful and some things have become a routine that we don't show appreciation for it like waking up, breathing, going to work, crossing streets and walking. It takes calamities, disasters and misfortunes of other people for us to appreciate these miracles in life. You need to consciously show gratitude for everything in life. You need to use your thanksgiving card at all times in all in situation. It works!

Inspired by Eugene Aikins

THANK YOU

I have come to say thank you

Two separate words, yet it seems thanks could never live a life without you.

Because thanks plus you comes together to connote the meaning,

'Am so grateful Lord, you are all I want and need'.

Thank you easily gets drowned in the sea of 'Lord I want this, Lord I want that'.

Thank you gets chased away when we choose to focus on what went wrong, and not on what went right.

Thank you is forgotten when we become absorbed in a world of normality, where we think that things are just as they should be and fail to recognise the power and the being behind this.

More disturbingly, thank you is forgotten because we choose to.

So Jesus asked the one leper who returned to give thanks:

'Were not all ten cleansed?'

An identification that God delights in thanksgiving.

Therefore, because I seek not just to be healed but to be made whole,

Like David, I enter his gates with thanksgiving and his courts with praise.

Thank you God for Mercy!

Your mercy that found me, that saved me from sin and from death;

Your mercy that dusted off me the filth and disgrace that this world would have me carry;

Your mercy that falls short of sentencing me to death, every time I falter and sin;

Your mercy that continues to give me renewed chances each passing day;

Your mercy that motivates you to continually plead on my behalf to the father;

Your mercy that says, even though you don't deserve it, I love you anyway;

Your mercy that has qualified me to stand here today, to stand before my father and proclaim 'Abba Father'.

Thank you God for Grace!

Your grace that is freely made available to me;

Your grace that comes with the knowledge that I can do all things through Christ who strengthens me;

Your grace that pushes me to press on despite the odds;

Your grace that has made me a giant to contend with, when in truth I might as well have been a dwarf.

Lord thank you for your grace in my academics and

your grace in my all.

Thank you God for Love!
The Greatest love mankind could ever experience.
Love so pure, so genuine, so overwhelming, so so so amazing.
I have yet to figure out the breadth and depth of this love, because the continued discovery of the height alone leaves me utterly speechless.
I could choose to describe your love but it is indescribable.
I could choose to tame your love but it is untamable
How is it possible that you could see the depths of my heart; the secrets in my closet that no one could imagine, much more know; the nitty gritty's of my wretched life inside and out and still love me the same? Oh my God, Oh my Jesus, such love for me is incomprehensible.

In 2013 Lord, had it not been your love for me
I know I would have failed,
I know I would have given up,
I know I would have been lost,
I know I would have died.

Thank you God for Faithfulness!
Whereas I chose to measure your faithfulness by the prayers you answered, you have steadily taught me to measure it by your nature.
Faithfulness is your nature; you could never be unfaithful because that would deny your nature.
So this I say, thank you God for unanswered prayers in 2013 because this way I know it's either you saved me from the wrong or you taught me to be patient as I await your right moment.

Thank you God for the times I cried, the times when only tears were the food I could have appetite for, because you taught me to trust you even when it seemed you were far off, you were silent and I could not see your hand.

Thank you God for problems.
Now I can appreciate that if I never had a problem, I would never know that you could solve them.

Yes God in 2013, I needed a job, but I am still jobless;
I needed a raise and a promotion, am still stunted in growth in my job;
I needed marriage, I am still single;
I needed a child, I am still childless.
However, thank you anyway. I will praise you in advance for I know that confuses the enemy.
I will praise you despite my pain and grief.
You are faithful beyond all this.

I am alive, Yes God I am alive to see your goodness in 2014.
Once more to experience your grace, your mercy, your love and your faithfulness in 2014.I am excited about tomorrow God, I am excited about 2014, I am excited beyond 2014, I am excited about my future simply God because you are in it.

Thank you God, thank you Jesus. Thank you Holy Spirit because I know when I found you. I found life. I love you Lord and I know I am a winner.

Copyright ~ Christine Ofosu-Ampadu ~ 30th December 2013

REFERENCES

1. Benny Hinn The Biblical Road to Blessings (Nashville, Thomas Nelson Inc, 1997), 31
2. http://en.wikipedia.org/wiki/Thanksgiving retrieved on October 14, 2013
3. http://prayerforsuccess.org/be-thankful/
4. http://www.brainyquote.com/quotes/quotes/h/henrywardb105506.html
5. http://www.brainyquote.com/quotes/quotes/s/saintaugus107689.html
6. http://www.goodreads.com/author/quotes/1153365.Harry_A_Ironside
7. http://www.goodreads.com/author/quotes/953666.John_Henry_Jowett
8. Neale Donald Walsch Conversations with God: an uncommon dialogue. Book 1(New York, The Berkley Publishing Corporation, 1997) May 12 Quote
9. S. J. Hill Enjoying God: Experiencing the Love of Your Heavenly Father (Florida, Charisma Media, 2012),